Praise for Super Ears

"The Author did a good job explaining the concepts at an age appropriate level. The book gave some good recommendations on strategies that kids can use to manage their condition. I think it will be a great resource for kids and families dealing with misophonia."

Erica Colt, Audiologist

Super Ears

My Misophonia Workbook

Megan Menkis ATR-BC, LPC

Super Ears

My Misophonia Workbook

Megan Menkis ATR-BC, LPC

MERAKI PRESS

PUBLISHING HOUSE

Additional copies may be purchased from Meraki Press.
Contact merakipress2021@gmail.com for information about bulk purchases or any other questions.

Cover Design: Sarah Vasquez
Illustrator: Megan Menkis
Layout Design: Katie Zeliger of Meraki Press

Printed in the U.S.A
First Edition: May 2023
ISBN: 979-8-9873516-3-5

Megan Menkis ATR-BC, LPC
malbohn@gmail.com

Megan Menkis is a Licensed Professional Counselor and Board Certified Art Therapist. She has been practicing in PA for over 5 years and has a passion for working with children and families.

Everyone's ears help them hear.
Everyone's ears are different.

Everyone has noises
they like and noises
they don't like.

Did you know that some
animals can even hear things
that human ears can't?

I have Misophonia.

Mispohonia is like having super ears,
because I can hear things
that other people don't notice.

Here is a list of things I can hear with my super ears

Did you know...

Misophonia means "the hatred of sound" - sounds that most people don't even notice can feel loud and frustrating to people who have Misophonia.

Sounds that can be hard for kids with Misophonia:

Chewing

Coughing

Slurping

Sniffing

... and more!

Having super ears can be hard.
When I hear something I don't like, my ears
send a message to my brain that makes my
brain go into "panic mode".

How do you feel when your
brain is in "panic mode"?

Draw Here

Everyone's brain goes into "panic mode" sometimes. It helps protect you when you are in danger.

If you saw a snake on a hike in the woods, you would want your brain to go into "panic mode" and tell you to run away!

What sends your brain into "panic mode"?

If you have Misophonia, the smallest noise can trick your brain into going into "panic mode".

Your brain thinks there is something dangerous or scary about a noise, even when there's not. This can be very confusing and upsetting for some kids.

Imagine having a fire drill at school...

The fire alarm goes off but you know there is no fire. When your brain goes into panic mode, it's like an alarm going off. Sometimes your brain gives you false alarms - only you don't always know its a false alarm!

The next part of the book has ideas for how you can notice your brain going into panic mode, and help turn that false alarm in your brain off.

Noises that send my brain
into panic mode:
(this book refers to those sounds
as "unpleasant")

1.

2.

3.

4.

5.

Hearing unpleasant noises can make me feel:

(circle all that apply)

Angry

Worried

Scared

Agitated

Annoyed

Sad

Frustrated

Alone

Different

Stuck

Unique

Stressed

Confused

Hurt

When I hear these noises,
this is what I do:
(circle all that apply)

Yelling   Running away

Screaming   Throwing

Crying   Stomping

Hitting   Breaking

_____   _____

This is how I feel in my body when my brain goes into "panic mode":

(circle all that apply)

Heart Pounding

Tight Muscles

Trouble Breathing

Hot and Sweaty

Jaw Clenched

_____

_____

This is how I look when
my brain is in "panic mode"

(Draw Here)

Misophonia is a Cycle

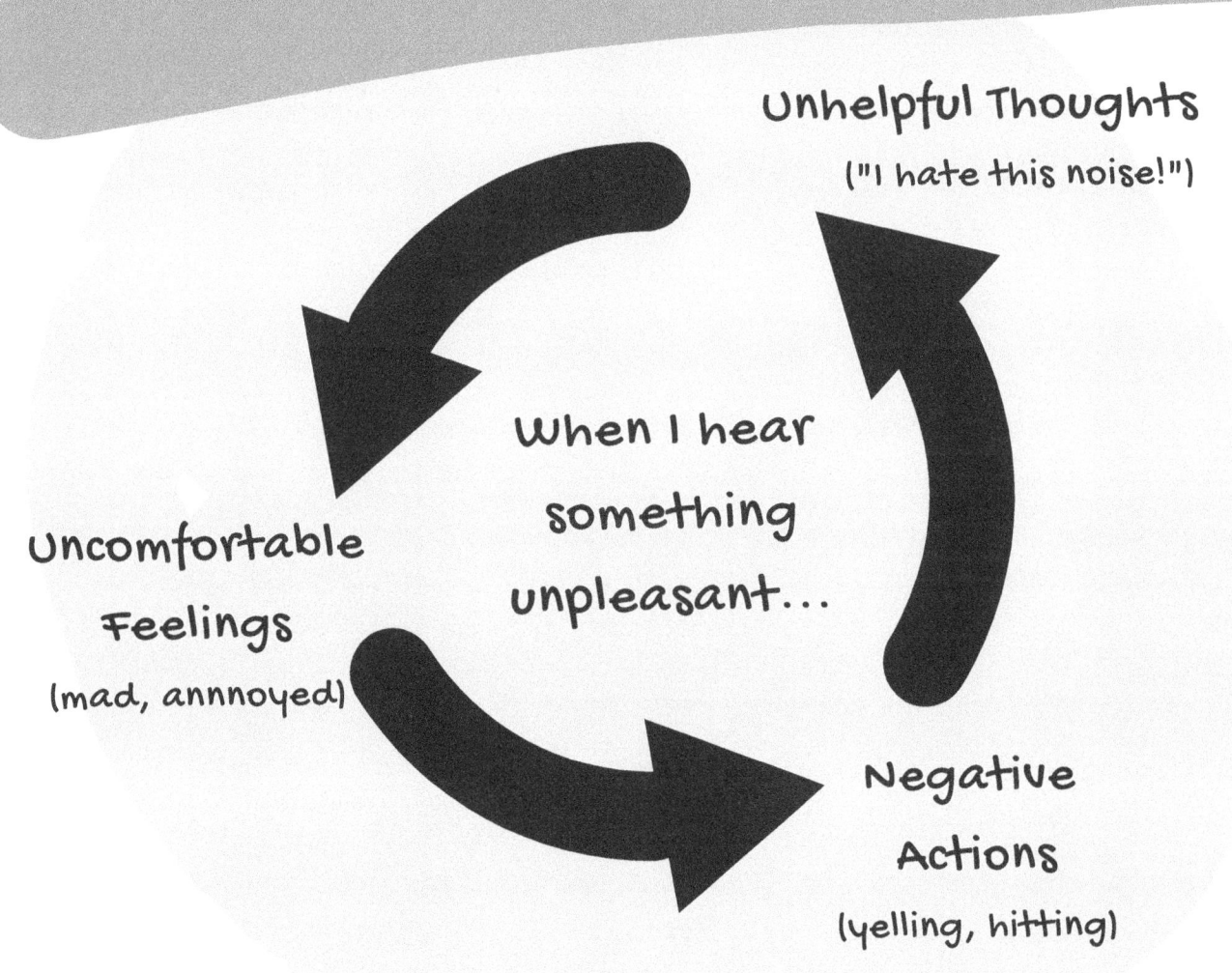

Unhelpful Thoughts
("I hate this noise!")

When I hear something unpleasant...

Uncomfortable Feelings
(mad, annnoyed)

Negative Actions
(yelling, hitting)

This is what my cycle looks like:

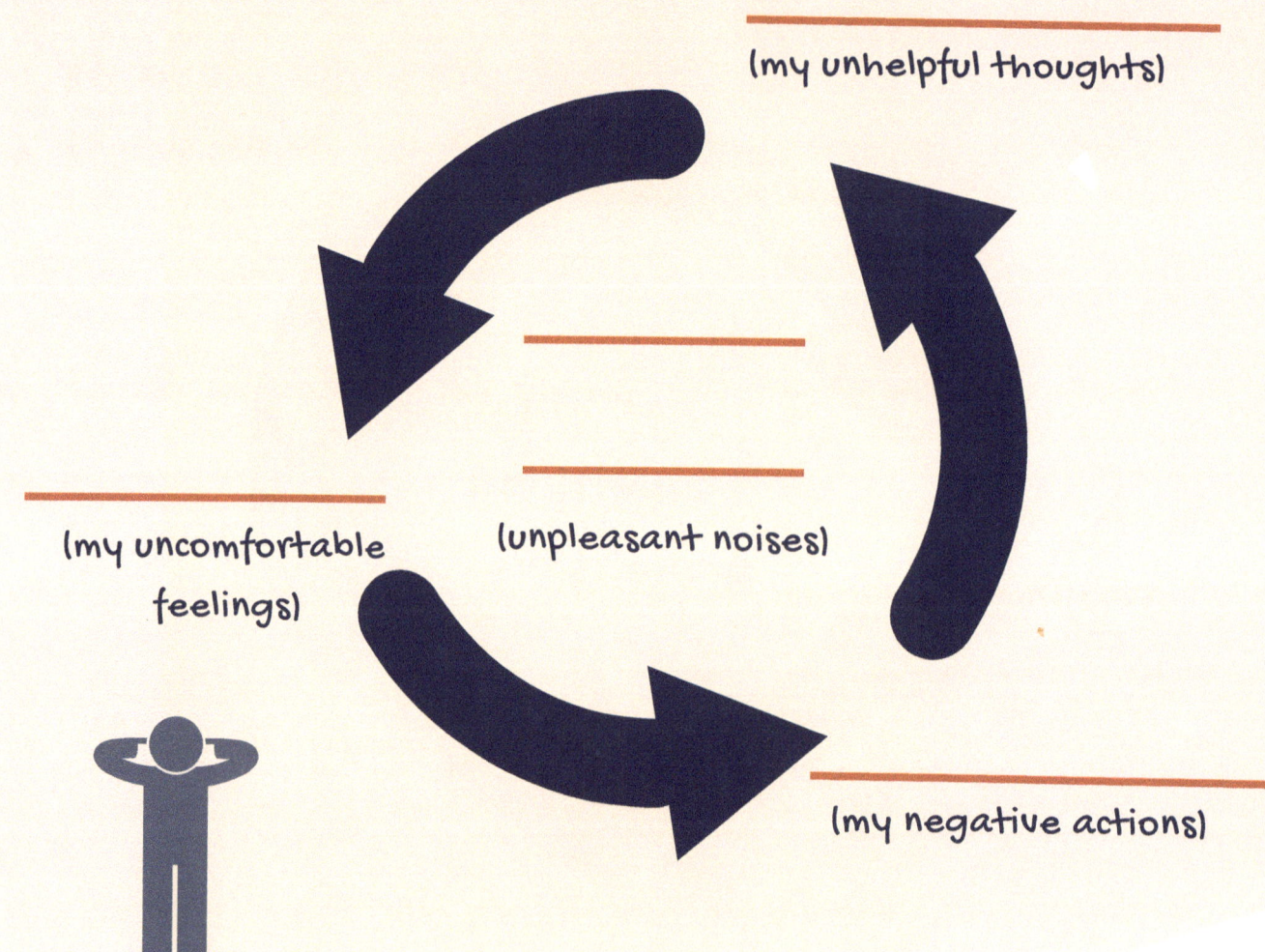

(my unhelpful thoughts)

(unpleasant noises)

(my uncomfortable feelings)

(my negative actions)

If my ears could talk, they would say...

If I could tell my ears one thing, I would say...

There's nothing wrong with my ears or my brain.
Everyone has noises they like and don't like.

I'm just more sensitive.

And that's ok.

When I hear unpleasant sounds, and my brain goes into "panic mode", I can try to remember something calm

A relaxing place

A peaceful thing

A list of noises that I like to hear:

1.

2.

3.

4.

5.

When I hear noises I don't like and my ears start to send unpleasant messages to my brain, I can try to close my eyes and imagine I hear these noises instead.

Some other things that help me
stay calm are...

More Calming Things:

(check the box if you are willing to try!)

- ☐ Wear noise cancelling headphones

- ☐ Hug a favorite stuffed animal or scream into a pillow

- ☐ Set up a calming area in the house with a few favorite things

- ☐ Write in a journal or draw a picture

- ☐ Close your eyes and take a few deep breaths as you count to 20

Some people might not understand why a noise bothers me so much, because their ears and brain don't work like mine.

That's ok, because I can explain Misophonia to them by telling them something simple, like...

I have super ears!

(insert your own ideas in the blank clouds)

Misophonia isn't the only thing about me. I am unique and special. Here are some other things about me.

1.

2.

3.

4.

5.

My Self-Portrait

Congratulations!

You completed the workbook.

Turn the page for some fun facts about hearing.

MORE FUN FACTS ABOUT HEARING:

Whales can communicate long distance - the shape of their skull bones amplify noise.

Elephants have the biggest ears of any mammal, and they can hear at such low frequencies that they can hear clouds rumble, which helps them to find water!

Bats use "echolocation" - which means they produce high-pitched sounds that bounce off what's around them, helping them to "see" better in the dark!

Humans have 6 different muscles in their ears that help them hear - cats have 32!

More Information

for Parents and Caregivers

TIPS FOR PARENTS:

While Misophonia is not yet recognized in the DSM-5, a growing body of research suggests that is it a neurological disorder. This means that the distress and discomfort caused by certain sounds is very real to your child - they are not just "being difficult" or "seeking attention." Their brain is going into "Fight or Flight" mode (or, panic mode as we call it in this book). The next page includes some tips on how you can best support your child who is struggling with Misophonia symptoms.

1. Try adding white noise or background noise to the room, it might help make the trigger less noticeable.
2. Practice progressive muscle relaxation or meditation with your child daily, to help them strengthen their ability to self-regulate.
3. Make a plan. Decide as a family how you will respond when triggers occur. With misophonia, prolonged exposure, or forcing your child to endure a trigger, may make symptoms worse.
4. Validate your child's feelings. Being triggered is not a choice for them - it is their brain perceiving danger and going directly to fight-or-flight mode.
5. Remain calm. When your child is feeling overwhelmed, they look to you for reassurance. Try to remain calm, cool, and collected.

Check out these resources for more information on Misophonia:

The Misophonia Institute
https://misophoniainstitute.org/

Misophonia International
https://www.misophoniainternational.com/

Duke Center for Misophonia Research and Education
https://www.misophonia.duke.edu/

Misophonia Education - Dr. Brout
https://www.misophoniainternational.com/author/dr-jennifer-jo-brout/

About the Author

Megan Menkis is a Licensed Professional Counselor and Board Certified Art Therapist. She has been practicing in PA for over 5 years and has a passion for working with children and families.

www.ingramcontent.com/pod-product-compliance
Lightning Source LLC
Chambersburg PA
CBHW041525120626
46551CB00018B/2570